MW00522893

# Teaching Vocabulary

## Lessons from the Corpus,
## Lessons for the Classroom

Jeanne McCarten

CAMBRIDGE
UNIVERSITY PRESS

CAMBRIDGE UNIVERSITY PRESS
Cambridge, New York, Melbourne, Madrid, Cape Town, Singapore, São Paulo

Cambridge University Press
32 Avenue of the Americas, New York, NY 10013-2473, USA

www.cambridge.org

© Cambridge University Press 2007

This book is in copyright. Subject to statutory exception
and to the provisions of relevant collective licensing agreements,
no reproduction of any part may take place without
the written permission of Cambridge University Press.

First published 2007

Printed in the United States of America

ISBN-13 978-0-521-94325-3 paperback

Book layout services: Page Designs International

# *Table of Contents*

# 1 | *Lessons from the Corpus*

## How many words are there and how many do we need to teach?

It's almost impossible to say exactly how many words there are in English. The Global Language Monitor, which tracks language trends, especially in the media, has counted up to almost a million at 988,968. *Webster's Third New International Dictionary, Unabridged,* together with its 1993 Addenda Section, includes around 470,000 entries.

Counting words is a complicated business. For a start, what do we mean by a word? Look at these members of the word family RUN: *run, runs, running, ran, runner,* and *runners.* Should we count these as one "word" or six? How do we count different uses of the same word? For example, is the verb *run* the same in *run a marathon* as in *run a company*? Is it the same as the noun *a run*? How do we deal with idiomatic uses like *run out of gas, feel run down,* or *a run of bad luck*? And, of course, new words are being added to the language all the time; the Internet especially has given us lots of new words like *podcast, netizen,* and *blog,* as well as new meanings such as *surf* as in *surf the web.*

Despite such difficulties, researchers have tried to estimate how many words native speakers know in order to assess the number of words learners need to learn. Estimates for native speakers vary between 12,000 and 20,000 depending on their level of education. One estimate is that a native speaker university graduate knows about 20,000 word families (Goulden, Nation, and Read, 1990), not including phrases and expressions. Current learners' dictionaries such as the *Cambridge Dictionary of American English* include "more than 40,000 frequently used words and phrases . . ." This huge number of items presents a challenge that would be impossible for most English language learners, and even for many native speakers.

Fortunately, it is possible to get along in English with fewer than 20,000 words. Another way of deciding the number of words learners need is to count how many different words are used in an average spoken or written text. Because some high-frequency words are repeated, it is said that learners can understand a large proportion of texts with a relatively small vocabulary. So, for example, learners who know the most frequent 2,000 words should be able to understand almost 80 percent of the words in an average text, and a knowledge of 5,000 words increases learners' understanding to 88.7 percent (Francis and Kucera 1982). For spoken language, the news is even better since about 1,800 words make up over 80 percent of the spoken corpus (McCarthy 2004;

O'Keeffe, McCarthy, and Carter 2007). While learning up to 5,000 words is still a challenge, it represents a much more achievable learning goal for most learners than 20,000 words.

So far there are two lessons to be learned from all of this. First, it seems important to identify what the most frequent 2,000 to 5,000 vocabulary items are and to give them priority in teaching. Second, students need to become self-sufficient learners. It is unlikely that teachers can cover in class the huge number of vocabulary items that students will need to use or understand, so it is equally important to help students with *how* to learn vocabulary as well as with *what* to learn.

## What can a corpus tell us about vocabulary?

### What is a corpus?

A corpus is basically a collection of texts which is stored in a computer. The texts can be written or spoken language. Written texts like newspapers and magazines can be entered into the computer from a scanner, a CD, or the Internet. Spoken texts, like conversations, are recorded and then the recordings are transcribed; that is, they are written down word for word, so that the texts of these conversations can be fed into the computer database. It is then possible to analyze the language in the corpus with corpus software tools to see how people really speak or write. [For more information, see Michael McCarthy's booklet *Touchstone: from Corpus to Course Book* (2004) in this series.]

### What kind of corpus do we need to use?

A large corpus is often divided into sections, or subcorpora, which contain different types of English. For example, there are subcorpora of different varieties such as North American English and British English, or different types of language like conversation, newspapers, business English, and academic English. To use a corpus in designing a syllabus, the first thing to decide is what kind of English we want to base our material on, because different corpora will give us different words and often different uses of words to teach. For example, the word *nice* is in the top fifteen words in conversation, but it is rare in written academic English, occurring mainly in quotations of speech from literature or interviews. Another example is the word *see,* which has the same frequency in conversation and written academic English, but different uses. In academic English, *see* is mostly used to refer the reader to other books and articles, as in *see McCarthy, 2004* – the way it was used at the end of the last paragraph. In conversation, *see* has a greater variety of uses including the expression *I see,* which means "I understand," and *See* and *You see,* which introduce what the speaker feels is new information for the listener, as in Example 1.

**Example 1**

Someone describes his relationship with his neighbors to a stranger:

*You see I have neighbors that I'm good friends with, as far as neighbor-wise.*

So our choice of corpus may affect which words we will include in our materials and which meanings of those words we will teach. For most students in general English courses, the priority is speaking, so for these students it makes sense to base much of the syllabus on a spoken corpus. Many students also have to write in English, especially for examinations, so again it makes sense to look at a corpus that includes the kinds of texts students will have to write. Most of the examples in this booklet are taken from conversations found in the North American spoken corpus, which is part of the *Cambridge International Corpus* (referred to as "the Corpus" hereafter).

So what can we learn from the Corpus about vocabulary? Essentially it can tell us about:

- **Frequency:** Which words and expressions are most frequent and which are rare
- **Differences in speaking and writing:** Which vocabulary is more often spoken and which is more often written
- **Contexts of use:** The situations in which people use certain vocabulary
- **Collocation:** Which words are often used together
- **Grammatical patterns:** How words and grammar combine to form patterns
- **Strategic use of vocabulary:** Which words and expressions are used to organize and manage discourse

Corpus tools help us analyze the huge amount of data in the Corpus, which can consist of millions of words. But in addition to providing the more statistical kinds of information (a **quantitative** analysis), the Corpus also gives us access to hundreds of texts which we can read in order to observe how people use vocabulary in context – a **qualitative** analysis. For example, it is possible to see what kinds of vocabulary people use to talk about a topic like music or celebrities, or how they repeat words, or avoid repeating words by using synonyms. The Corpus, however, cannot tell us exactly what to teach or how to teach, and it has nothing to tell us with respect to how students learn best. It cannot replace the expertise of teachers, or of students themselves, on how best to teach and learn vocabulary. It is *a* tool. It is not the *only* tool.

# Frequency

A list from the Corpus of the most frequently used words can give us lots of interesting information about the spoken language (see Appendix). *I* is the most common word; the five most common verbs (apart from parts of the verbs *be* and *have*) are *know, think, get, go,* and *mean*; the most common nouns are *people, time,* and *things*; the most common adjective is *good*. We can also see which words are more common than similar or related words: *Yeah* is more frequent than *yes*; *little* is more frequent than *small*; some plurals like *things, years, kids,* and *children* are more frequent than the singular forms (*thing, year,* etc.). The list raises questions such as: Why are the adverbs *just* and *actually* more frequent than grammatical items like *doesn't*? Why is *something* more frequent than *anything, everything,* and *nothing*?

How can we use this information in teaching materials? Frequency lists are useful to help us make choices about what to teach and in what order. For example, we can see that many idioms are rare, so we can teach them later in the language program. On the other hand, we can see which items in a large vocabulary set (colors, types of music, clothing, health problems, etc.) people talk about most and teach those first, leaving the less frequent words until later. The way that frequency information is used in corpus-informed materials can be almost invisible, but some of this frequency information is fun to know and can be used in guessing game activities in class. For example, have students guess what weather expressions people in North America use most (*It's cold, It's hot*) or ask them to brainstorm a list of clothing that can be used with the phrase *a pair of*, then guess which are most frequent (*shoes* and *pants*).

So, in a basic course, should we teach all the words in the top 2,000 word list and in the order in which they appear? It may not be possible to use all the items in the list, for a number of reasons. Some may be culturally inappropriate, not suitable for class, or just difficult to use until students have more English. Also, the communication needs of students may be different from those of the people whose conversations are recorded in the Corpus. For example, a word like *homework*, a frequent word in any classroom, comes toward the end of the top 2,000 words, whereas words like *supposed, true,* and *already*, which are in the top 400, might be challenging for elementary learners. Frequency information, while important, is only a guide.

## Differences in speaking and writing

Corpus tools can give us information about how frequent a word is in different corpora, so we can compare the frequency of vocabulary in, say, newspapers, academic texts, and conversation. For example, the word *probably* is about five times more frequent in conversation than in newspapers and ten times more frequent in conversation than in academic texts. On the other hand, *however* is eight times more frequent in newspapers than in conversation and over twenty times more frequent in academic texts than in conversation. Looking at such differences, we can see whether to present vocabulary items like these in a written or spoken context.

## Contexts of use

The Corpus includes information about speakers and situations in which conversations take place. It is possible to see, for example, whether an item of vocabulary is used by everyone in all kinds of situations, or mostly by people who know each other very well, or mostly in more polite situations with strangers or work colleagues, etc. Information like this from the Corpus enables us to present vocabulary appropriately and to point out to students examples of more formal usage such as *Goodbye* vs. *Bye* and, perhaps more importantly, very informal usage such as using the word *like* for reporting speech (*I was like "Hey!"*) or the expression *and stuff* (*We have a lot of parties and stuff*).

## Collocation

The term **collocation** generally refers to the way in which two or more words are typically used together. For example, we talk about *heavy rain* but not *heavy sun*, or we say that we *make* or *come to a decision*, but we don't *do a decision*. So, *heavy rain* and *make a decision* are often referred to as **collocations** and we say that *heavy* **collocates with** *rain*, or that *heavy* and *rain* are **collocates** of each other. With collocation software we can search for all the collocates of a particular word, that is, all the words that are used most frequently with that word and especially those with a higher than anticipated frequency.

This is particularly useful for finding the collocates of verbs like *have*, *get*, *make*, and *do*, which are often referred to as *delexical verbs*. These are verbs which don't have a (lexical) meaning of their own, but take their meaning from the words that they collocate or are used with. For example, the verb *make* has a different meaning in each of the expressions *make a cake*, *make a decision*, and *make fun of*, so it is sensible to teach verbs like these in expressions, as collocations, instead of trying to identify and distinguish basic meanings, which is difficult and, in many cases, almost impossible.

Figure 1 shows some of the most frequent collocates of the words *make* and *do*. They include words that come immediately after the word (*make sure*) and words that come two or more words after it (***make a difference, make a huge mistake***).

> **MAKE:** *sure, difference, sense, decision, mistakes, decisions, money, judgments, mistake, reservations, copies, effort*
>
> **DO:** *anything, something, things, job, well, nothing, work, whatever, aerobics, gardening, stuff, homework, laundry*

**Figure 1:** Collocates of the words *make* and *do*.

Notice that although *make* is a frequent word, it collocates most strongly with a higher-level, lower-frequency vocabulary. On the other hand, the collocates of *do* are a mixture of very concrete, elementary items (*homework, laundry*) and more advanced abstract or vague vocabulary (*anything, something, things*). Lists like these help us make choices about what to teach at different levels.

At higher levels collocations can be taught and practiced overtly and students can be encouraged to write down collocations as well as single words. But even at the elementary level we can introduce the idea of words and expressions that are "used together" even if we do not use terms like collocation or collocates, and we can encourage students to keep notes of these in their vocabulary notebooks (see Figure 2).

Think of words and expressions that go with these verbs.

| GO | PLAY | READ |
|---|---|---|
|  |  |  |
|  |  |  |

**Figure 2:** Example of an elementary level collocation exercise.

## Grammatical patterns

### The grammar of vocabulary

The Corpus can show us the grammatical patterns that vocabulary forms – or the **grammar of vocabulary**. This is very helpful with verb complements, i.e., items and structures that must follow or that usually follow any particular verb, such as objects or infinitive verbs. It can answer questions about what forms are used after certain verbs when our intuition fails us. Let's take the example of questions with the verb *mind: Do you mind . . . ?* and *Would you mind . . . ?* Without looking at a corpus, four basic patterns seem equally possible:

| *Requests* | *Example* |
|---|---|
| Do you mind + . . . ing | *Do you mind helping me for a second?* |
| Would you mind + . . . ing | *Would you mind helping me for a second?* |

| *Asking for permission* | *Example* |
|---|---|
| Do you mind + if | *Do you mind if I leave early today?* |
| Would you mind + if | *Would you mind if I leave (or left) early today?* |

However, when we look at the phrases *Would you mind* and *Do you mind* in the Corpus, we find that two of these patterns stand out as being more frequent. Figure 3 includes a representative selection of examples of these phrases from the Corpus. Each phrase is shown in a **concordance**. A concordance is a screen display of a word or phrase as it is used by many different speakers in the Corpus. The word or phrase we are interested in is shown in the middle of the screen, highlighted in some way, with the rest of the text – if any – before and after it. So, in Figure 3, each line is someone speaking and using the phrase *Would you mind* or *Do you mind*.

**Would you mind** taking that day?
**Would you mind?**
bus driver said "**Would you mind** taking the seat by the window because he
**Would you mind** seeing if Nick wants cake Joel?
**Would you mind** . . .
**Would you mind** talking to us just for a minute?
**Would you mind?**
**Would you mind?**
the person says "**Would you mind** signing this form?"
And I was like "**Would you mind** driving us to Norris?"
**Would you mind** me asking what kind of dog is this?
**Would you mind** answering a couple of questions real qui

**Do you mind** if I grab this?
**Do you mind** if I go get a drink first?
She's like "**Do you mind?**"
**Do you mind** if I put some makeup on real quick?
**Do you mind?**
**Do you mind** if I uh take the um apple juice in the car?
**Do you mind** if I take these pretzels?
**Do you mind?**
**Do you mind** if I take a picture of your chocolates?
**Do you mind** us taping it?"
**Do you mind** if there's like white?
**Do you mind** if I put the thing on there?

**Figure 3:** Concordances of *Would you mind* and *Do you mind* from the Cambridge International Corpus, North American Conversation.

In some cases these phrases are used on their own as questions with no text following. Where the speaker continues, notice that *Do you mind* is mostly used in the expression *Do you mind if I* . . . to ask permission to do something. However, *Would you mind* is mostly used as *Would you mind* + . . . *ing* to ask other people to do something. Notice also the more complex patterns with an object (*Would you mind **me** asking* . . . and *Do you mind **us** taping* . . .) are also much less frequent. So we can make students' lives a little easier and teach the frequent patterns first, leaving the complex structures until a later level.

### The vocabulary of grammar

In addition to seeing the grammar of individual words – the grammar of vocabulary – we can also learn about the vocabulary used with certain grammar structures – the **vocabulary of grammar**. For example, the Corpus can tell us the most frequent verbs used in the past continuous structure *was . . . ing*. The top ten are *going, thinking, talking, doing, saying, trying, telling, wondering, looking, working*.

Notice that five of these verbs describe "saying" and "thinking." In addition, 12 percent of the uses of *was going to* are in the phrases *was going to say* or *was going to ask,* and 28 percent of the uses of *was trying* are with similar verbs of saying and thinking. So it seems that these verbs are an important part of the vocabulary of this structure. [See Carter and McCarthy (1995), which describes this as one aspect of the grammar of speech.] Shouldn't we then teach this vocabulary with this structure if we want students to learn the kind of usage they will hear from expert users and native speakers?

## Strategic vocabulary

Teachers are familiar with the kinds of words and expressions that writers use strategically to organize written texts, from simple conjunctions like *and* and *however,* which organize ideas within and across sentences, and adverbs such as *first, secondly,* etc., which list ideas within a paragraph or text, to expressions such as *in conclusion,* which signal that the text is about to end. Written texts are easy to find in newspapers, books, on the Internet, etc., as models for teaching or our own writing. But what is the strategic vocabulary that speakers use to organize and manage conversations, and how can we find it? To help us answer these questions, we need a corpus so we can analyze many different conversations. We can start by looking again at frequency lists to identify and analyze the kind of strategic vocabulary speakers use.

In addition to looking at single words, we can ask the Corpus to give us frequency lists of phrases – vocabulary items that contain more than one word, sometimes called "chunks," "lexical bundles," or "clusters" [see McCarthy and Carter (2002); O'Keeffe, McCarthy, and Carter (2007)]. These lists contain "fragments," or bits of language that don't have a meaning as expressions in their own right, such as *in the, and I,* and *of the.* However, we can remove these to find expressions that do have their own meaning, as in Figure 4.

| No. of words in phrase | Examples |
|---|---|
| two | *you know, I mean, I guess, or something* |
| three | *a little bit, and all that* |
| four | *or something like that, and things like that* |
| five | *you know what I mean, as a matter of fact* |
| six | *it was nice talking to you; and all that kind of stuff* |
| seven+ words | *a lot of it has to do (with)* . . . |

**Figure 4:** Expressions from frequency lists in the Cambridge International Corpus, North American Conversation.

Some of these expressions are much more frequent than the everyday, basic, single words that we would expect to teach at an elementary level. Chunks such as *I mean, I don't know,* and *or something* are more frequent than words like *woman, six,* and *black.* This suggests we need to take chunks seriously as vocabulary items to teach in a basic course.

### Finding a vocabulary of conversation

When we look at the most frequent words and phrases in conversation, we find many items that conversation shares with the written language, such as grammatical words (articles, pronouns, prepositions, etc.), common everyday nouns, verbs, adjectives, and adverbs (*people, money, go, see, different, interesting, still, usually*), and modal items (*can, should, maybe, probably*). As we saw earlier, some of these may be far more frequent in conversation than in writing (e.g., *probably*) or have different uses (e.g., *see*).

In addition to these grammatical and common everyday words and phrases, we also find items that distinguish the spoken language from the written, items that reflect the interactive nature of conversation and that give conversation its distinctive character. We can perhaps best describe these as a **vocabulary of conversation** rather than merely as vocabulary *in* conversation. Below are examples of the types of this vocabulary with extracts from the Corpus to show how people have actually used them. Note that some of the frequent expressions have several uses and fall into more than one category.

### Discourse markers

A **discourse marker** is a word or phrase that organizes or manages the discourse in some way. In this case the type of discourse is conversation. Some of these expressions help organize the conversation as a whole, and some organize the speaker's own speech. Examples include *anyway,* which speakers use (often with words like *so* or *well*) to come back to the main point after a digression or interruption, as in Example 2.

---

**Example 2**

Speaker A gets back to the main point of her story, using *anyway.*

A: *[. . .] I won first prize.*
B: *Oh you always win.*
A: *I don't win.*
B: *Yes you do.*
A: *And so **anyway** the prize was ten dollars . . .*

---

*Anyway* is also used to show that a conversation is coming to an end:

---

**Example 3**

*Well, **anyway**. Gotta run.*

---

Speakers organize their own speech; an example is the expression *I mean,* which signals the speaker is going to restate, repeat, clarify, or add to what was just said.

---

**Example 4**

Here the speaker uses *I mean* to explain what she means by "pretty much grown":

*[. . .] this is home for my kids now. Um they're pretty much grown. **I mean** they're nineteen and seventeen.*

---

Speakers also have ways of highlighting and emphasizing the main points of what they want to say with expressions such as *the point is* or *the thing is* and variations like *the only thing is* or *the funny/weird thing is* to show their attitude toward what they will say.

---

**Example 5**

Here speaker A makes the main point of her news about a publishing project using the expression *the thing is*:

A: *[. . .] they want to really publish it.*

B: *Wow.*

A: *So but I mean* **the thing is** *they want the completed manuscript in a month.*

*Responses*

Very frequent on the list are words and expressions that people use to react or respond to what other people say, before they add their own contribution to the conversation. These include expressions to show agreement (*Exactly, Absolutely, That's true*); expressions to show understanding (*I know, I know what you mean, I see*); reactions to good or bad news (*Great!, That's nice, That's too bad*), or expressions which simply show the listener is still listening and participating in the conversation (*Uh huh, Mmm, Yeah, Huh*).

*Monitoring expressions*

In conversation, speakers often involve the other participants to measure how the conversation is going. For example, a speaker may use expressions like *you know what I mean*, or the shorter *you know*, to check if others in the conversation understand, sympathize with, or even agree with what he or she is saying. These expressions can create the impression that the speaker feels the listener shares his or her view or knowledge of the topic. In contrast, expressions such as *you see, let me tell you*, and *actually* create the opposite impression that the speaker is "telling" the listener something that he or she may not already know. These strategies are not just luxuries or optional extras, but they are important in creating true *dialogue* and in creating good relationships between the people involved in the conversation. [See Carter and McCarthy (2006), secs. 109 and 505c, for more on this topic.]

*Vague expressions*

Related to the idea outlined above about monitoring shared knowledge and views, a large number of expressions fall into a category which linguists call **vague language**. These include expressions that use very general, often informal words, instead of specific words to refer to things, activities, or situations. Some of the most frequent are the phrases *or something, and things like that, and stuff, and everything, or whatever, and that kind of thing*, and *and that sort of stuff*. More formal examples are *and so on, and so forth*, and *etcetera*. These expressions basically mean "I don't need to say this in detail because I think you know what I'm saying."

Following are some examples of these expressions in extracts from the Corpus.

---

**Example 6**

Someone talking about the fall season:

*... the trees are turning different colors and it's nice to walk around and the state parks are nice and it's nice to go out to a restaurant **or something** you know like for a snack **or something like that**.*

---

**Example 7**

Someone talking about shoes:

*Like they're more for outdoor running **and stuff like that**.*

---

**Example 8**

Someone describing an aunt:

*She's very sophisticated and she travels **and things like that**.*

---

The examples above show how these expressions can refer to a range of items including places (Example 6: *a restaurant*), things (Example 6: *a snack*), and activities (Example 7: *running* and Example 8: *travels*). They are versatile expressions that are not restricted by conventional grammar rules. For example, *or something* can refer back to singular and plural nouns, adjectives, adverbs, and verbs. The expression *and stuff* with its non-count noun *stuff* mostly follows plural count nouns (*what about sweaters and stuff?*), and the plural *and things* can follow singular and non count nouns (*I can call him up for advice and things*), as well as verbs.

Conversation is full of these (and other) types of vague expressions and it would be very difficult to communicate without them. For one thing, it would be highly impractical for speakers to list all the things they are thinking of – and probably boring to listen to – while removing them completely might sound pedantic or blunt. [See Carter and McCarthy (2006), secs. 103 and 505d, for more on vague expressions.]

*Hedging expressions*

Speakers use hedging expressions when they want to avoid sounding blunt, too direct, too sure of themselves, or too "black and white." [See Carter and McCarthy (2006), secs. 112 and 146c.] These expressions can introduce shades of gray, give the speaker a chance to go back and modify something he or she said earlier, and allow the listener to challenge or question what the speaker says. They include expressions such as *kind of, sort of, just, I guess, a little, in a way, probably* and speakers often use more than one in the same sentence. Below are examples of speakers using some of these expressions in a variety of situations.

---

### Example 9

Someone talking about her new boyfriend; she uses *kind of* and *sort of* to "soften" the adjectives, to sound less unequivocal or precise.

*He's very smart but he's also **kind of** young and naïve and quiet and **sort of** shy.*

---

### Example 10

Someone leaves a voicemail message for a friend; he uses *just* to show that the reason for his call isn't too important or urgent. This act of "downtoning" an invitation or suggestion makes it sound less coercive or restricting for the listener.

*I was **just** wondering if you were up for Chinese dinner tonight before bowling so give me a buzz if you're around.*

---

### Example 11

Here a speaker uses hedges when a "yes" or "no" answer isn't possible:

*A: Do you still live with your family?*
*B: Uh **sort of**, **in a way**.*

Hedging is very useful in situations where it is important to be "polite," for example, in stores and restaurants. Notice in Example 12 how the customer uses more than one hedge.

---

### Example 12

In a restaurant:

*Server:      Would you like cream in it?*
*Customer: **Just a little bit, I guess**.*

Hedging expressions can also be found in conversations when speakers feel they may be imposing on someone – even friends or family:

---

**Example 13**

A request in a family conversation:

A: *Could you do me a favor?*

B: *Yeah.*

A: *That glass thing. Could you **just** put it back out on the um . . . the table out there.*

---

*Expressions of stance*

Stance refers to how speakers express their attitude to what they say. So, for example, they may give information as a personal opinion and use expressions like *personally, I think, from my point of view*, etc. Sometimes they present information as facts about which they are very certain with words and phrases like *definitely, in fact, as a matter of fact*, or less certain using *maybe, probably, I don't know, I'm not sure*. Sometimes they want to assure the listener they are being truthful: *to be honest (with you)*. And of course speakers express an emotional response to what they say with expressions like *Unfortunately, I would hate to, the awful thing was*. [See Carter and McCarthy (2006), sec. 111, for more on stance.]

## Teaching strategic vocabulary: Fundamentals for a syllabus

How can this kind of strategic language be fitted into language materials? It is best taught in the context of teaching conversation strategies and skills. By categorizing the types of expressions and observing the kinds of strategies that speakers in the Corpus use to manage and conduct conversations, it is possible to construct a conversation syllabus that includes this vocabulary of conversation. The syllabus can be built around four broad functional areas that we find in all successful conversations in the Corpus:

- Organizing your own talk
- Taking account of another speaker
- Showing listenership, that is, showing you understand by responding appropriately [see O'Keeffe, McCarthy, and Carter (2007)]
- Managing the conversation as a whole

Mastery of these four aspects of conversation helps speakers, and therefore learners, to participate in and manage successful, fluent conversations.

*Organizing your own talk*

This area includes strategies such as giving your own views and opinions, highlighting key points, taking time to think, correcting yourself, or simply keeping a turn in the conversation. This area of the syllabus can also include how speakers use vocabulary to repeat their ideas, as exemplified in the extract shown in Figure 5 from a textbook conversation modeled on a Corpus conversation.

> *Nicole:* [. . .] I have some strange dreams.
> *Carlos:* You do? I hardly ever dream.
> *Nicole:* Yeah. I um . . . I've had some weird dreams. Really weird dreams. And they're scary. They're always scary ones. They're never good ones. They're just weird and off the wall.

**Figure 5:** Extract from a textbook conversation showing vocabulary repetition. (From *Touchstone*.)

The speaker uses synonyms to repeat her main ideas: ***strange dreams . . . weird dreams . . . weird and off the wall***. Some words (*weird* and *scary*) are repeated but intensified, the meaning is made stronger the second time: *some weird dreams . . . **really** weird dreams; they're scary . . . they're **always** scary*. Then the idea of bad dreams is repeated with a negative word and an opposite: *they're never good ones*. Practicing this kind of vocabulary use can make students not only sound more natural and fluent, but helps them to learn and exploit vocabulary skills of using synonyms and opposites, instead of just making lists of synonyms and opposites which they may never actually use.

*Taking account of another speaker*

This area of the syllabus includes ways of being polite, not offending other people, or not being too direct. For example, when people want to reply to a question with a "no" answer, they often choose to say *not really*, which is softer.

Other strategic vocabulary we can include are expressions like *you know, you know what I mean, I don't know if (you . . .)*, to appeal to common ground, or the vague expressions *or something (like that), and stuff, and that kind of thing*, which we looked at earlier. These expressions create the impression that the speaker assumes the listener will understand what he or she means or will know what he or she is referring to. In this way they project shared knowledge.

Figure 6 is an extract from an exercise that practices some vague expressions which students have seen and heard already.

What do the vague expressions mean in these conversations? Choose two ideas from the box for each one.

| | |
|---|---|
| anniversaries | folk songs |
| candles | holidays |
| concerts | see old friends |
| cultural events | sing "Happy Birthday" |
| dancing | spend time at home |

1. *A:* Do you go to a restaurant to celebrate birthdays *and stuff*?
   *B:* Yeah, we know a nice place. They bring out cakes *and everything*.

**Figure 6:** Extract from an exercise practicing vague expressions. (From *Touchstone*.)

### Showing listenership

This area of the syllabus includes a range of responses, from acknowledgements that the listener is engaged and indeed listening (*Huh, uh-huh*, etc.) to responses with more content, such as *that's right, wonderful, that would be* (*nice*), etc. In this way, the listener does more than just listen silently and process the message; he or she is an active and engaged listener, displaying what we call good "listenership." Even at the elementary level students can practice responding to good and bad news using a limited number of expressions with *that's* plus an adjective, as in Figure 7, below.

Complete the responses using an expression with *That's*.

*A:* I'm taking a karate class. We have a great teacher.
*B:* Oh, _____
[Possible answers: *that's nice, that's great*]

**Figure 7:** Practice idea for expressions with *That's* + adjective in responses. (From *Touchstone*.)

### *Managing the conversation as a whole*

This area of the syllabus includes opening conversations or starting new topics (*so, now*) and ending conversations (*anyway, all right*), going back to earlier topics (*as you were saying, going back to what you were saying*), interrupting and restarting conversations (*Hold on a sec, where were we?*). Many of these conversational functions can be realized with vocabulary that is well within the grasp of learners up to the intermediate level.

# 2 | *Lessons for the Classroom*

## What do we need to teach about vocabulary?

In Part 1 we have seen that learning vocabulary is a challenge for learners, partly because of the size of the task, and partly because of the variety of vocabulary types to be learned, including single words, phrases, collocations, and strategic vocabulary, as well as grammatical patterning, idioms, and fixed expressions. Richards (1976) and Nation (2001) list the different things learners need to know about a word before we can say that they have learned it. These include:

- The meaning(s) of the word
- Its spoken and written forms
- What "word parts" it has (e.g., any prefix, suffix, and "root" form)
- Its grammatical behavior (e.g., its word class, typical grammatical patterns it occurs in)
- Its collocations
- Its register
- What associations it has (e.g., words that are similar or opposite in meaning)
- What connotations it has
- Its frequency

To these we could add whether a word has a strategic use and if it has any special uses that are different in registers such as conversation or academic writing. So we can already see how important it is to use a corpus in order to give our learners all the right information they might need to master a word or phrase.

It would be unrealistic to teach everything there is to know about a word the first time it is presented to students – and any such attempt would make for some very tedious lessons. Obviously we need to make choices about how much we teach on a first presentation. For example with the word *like*, in addition to its sound and spelling we might choose to teach only one of its meanings (to enjoy, find something to be pleasant), with one grammatical pattern (*I like* + singular or plural noun) and some associated vocabulary (*I like football/cartoons; I can't stand game shows*). At a later date we can add other meanings such as to be similar to (*I have a car like that*) or add more grammatical patterns such as *like* + *to* + verb (*I like to play tennis*). The choices we make are influenced by factors such as frequency, usefulness for the classroom, and "learnability" – how easy the item is to learn (and teach!).

We can also take each type of knowledge from the list above and make students aware of its importance and usefulness in building up their knowledge of a word. For example, we can focus occasionally on how to express opposite or similar meanings for a set of vocabulary we are teaching, show students what is useful to learn about the forms of nouns or verbs, or how prefixes and suffixes can help build vocabulary knowledge quickly. Giving students practice in manipulating these different areas of knowledge teaches useful learning strategies they can apply to learning other vocabulary. We should also encourage students to look at learning the various meanings of an item of vocabulary as a gradual, incremental process, and show them how they can come back to a word they have previously "learned" to add more information about it, such as other meanings, or how to create an opposite meaning using a prefix. [See Schmitt (2000).]

Another issue to consider is which vocabulary we want students to be able to use when they speak and write (their **active** or **productive** vocabulary) and which we want them to be able to recognize and understand but not necessarily produce (their **passive** or **receptive** vocabulary). [See Melka (1997).] Students often feel frustrated that they can understand more than they can produce, but explaining this issue of active versus passive knowledge as a normal part of learning can be reassuring. When you assign vocabulary lists to learn, why not include some passive vocabulary items and discuss with students which items they need to learn "for understanding" and which they need to learn really well so that they can use them. (But be sure that in practice or testing activities, students are required to remember and use only the active vocabulary productively.)

Additionally, even from the elementary level, it is important to include in vocabulary lessons not just single words, but also larger "chunks" such as collocations, phrases, or expressions, even whole sentences, as well as strategic vocabulary [see Sökmen (1997)]. By building up a stock of expressions as well as individual words, students can assemble the language they need to communicate more fluently.

## How can we help learners learn vocabulary?

As we said earlier, there is a lot to learn about vocabulary in terms of its range, the sheer number of words and phrases to learn, and the depth of knowledge students need to know about each vocabulary item. Materials can help students in two broad areas: First, they need to present and practice in natural contexts the vocabulary that is frequent, current, and appropriate to learners' needs. Second, materials should help students become better learners of vocabulary by teaching different techniques and strategies they can use to continue learning outside the classroom. There is a vast amount of research into how learners learn best and how teachers might best teach. The next section presents some key principles that we can follow to help students learn vocabulary more effectively.

### Teaching vocabulary in class

#### Focus on vocabulary

Give vocabulary a high profile in the syllabus and the classroom so that students can see its importance and understand that learning a language isn't just about learning grammar (O'Dell 1997). It may be worth teaching students an easier formulation of Wilkins's (1972) view that "without grammar very little can be conveyed, without vocabulary nothing can be conveyed."

One of the first vocabulary learning strategies for any classroom is how to ask for words you don't know in English, and how to ask the meaning of English words you don't understand, so phrases like "What's the word for _____ in English?," "How do you say _____?," and "What does _____ mean?" are useful to teach at the basic levels. As students progress, another useful strategy they can use is to paraphrase: "It's a kind of _____," "It's like a _____," and "It's for _____-ing X" etc. Focusing on these strategies puts vocabulary learning firmly on the classroom agenda.

An important vocabulary acquisition strategy which Nation (2001) calls "noticing" is seeing a word as something to be learned. In this view, knowing what to learn is a necessary prerequisite to learning. Teachers can help learners get into the habit of noticing by making clear in classroom instruction and homework assignments: which items should be learned, what each item is (a single word, a phrase, a collocation etc.) and for what purpose (active use or passive recognition). And materials can help teachers in this in the following ways:

- Providing clearly marked vocabulary lessons
- Making the target vocabulary set stand out, including focused practice and regular review
- Giving lists of vocabulary to be learned for the lesson

Structured vocabulary notebook exercises which are designed to make students focus on a particular vocabulary set or feature are a good way of developing this noticing strategy.

#### Offer variety

Tomlinson (1998) suggests a number of principles for developing successful materials. The first of these is that "Materials should achieve impact." He suggests that this can be done with unusual and appealing content, attractive presentations, and variety. Teachers can use different ways to present vocabulary including pictures, sounds, and different text types with which students can identify: stories, conversations, web pages, questionnaires, news reports, etc. In each of these contexts, topics should be relevant to students' interests. Similarly, practice activities should vary and engage students at different levels. These should range from simple listen-and-repeat type of practice through controlled practice to opportunities to use the vocabulary in meaningful, personalized ways. Offering variety also means catering to different learning styles, and as Tomlinson notes, some students may use different learning styles for different types of language or in different learning situations. So this means offering activities that sometimes appeal to learners who are more "studial" and "analytic" (those who need to analyze the language and to be accurate in their use of it) as well as learners who are "experiential" and "global" (those who are less concerned with accuracy as with learning whole chunks of language) and catering to students who prefer to learn either by seeing, hearing, or doing something.

## Repeat and recycle

Learning vocabulary is largely about remembering, and students generally need to see, say, and write newly learned words many times before they can be said to have learned them. Some researchers have suggested various numbers of encounters with a word for learning to take place, ranging from five to up to twenty [see, e.g., Nation (1990); Rott (1999); Ghadirian (2002)]. Some suggest that an impressive amount of learning can take place when students learn lists of paired items (English word and translation equivalents); others suggest that this method of learning does not aid deeper understanding of the words or help develop fluency. However, most agree that repetition is an important aid to learning and that having to actively recall or "retrieve" a word is a more effective way of learning than simple exposure or just seeing a word over and over (Sökmen 1997). Researchers also agree that repeating words aloud helps students remember words better than repeating them silently. Another area of research is how long students can remember words after first learning them, and again researchers agree that forgetting mostly occurs immediately after we first learn something, and that the rate of forgetting slows down afterward [see Gu (2003)]. The implications for the vocabulary classroom are self-evident: Review vocabulary as often as possible in activities that have students actively recall words and produce them rather than merely see or hear them.

## Provide opportunities to organize vocabulary

Organizing vocabulary in meaningful ways makes it easier to learn (Schmitt 1997; Sökmen 1997). Textbooks often present new vocabulary in thematic sets as an aid to memory, but there are other types of organization and these can be described under three broad headings: real-world groups, language-based groups, and personalized groups, examples of which are given below.

- **Real-world groups** occur in the real world, such as the countries within each continent, parts of the body, the foods in each food type (carbohydrate, protein, fats, etc.), activities that take place for a celebration (e.g., at a wedding), expressions people typically use in everyday situations (e.g., when someone passes an examination, has bad luck, etc.). Students can draw on their general knowledge to group English vocabulary according to concepts with which they are already familiar.

- **Language-based groups** draw on linguistic criteria as ways of grouping, for example, the different parts of speech of a word family; words that have the same prefix or suffix, or the same sound; verbs and dependent prepositions; collocations of different kinds (verb + noun; adjective + noun, etc.).

- **Personalized groups** use students' own preferences and experiences as the basis for the groups. It might include grouping vocabulary according to likes and dislikes, personal habits or personal history, for example, foods that you like and don't like, or eat often, sometimes, rarely, or that you ate for breakfast, lunch, and dinner yesterday. Making vocabulary personal helps to make it more memorable.

There are many different ways of practicing newly presented vocabulary in class, from repeating the words, controlled practice, or reacting to the content in some way, to using the vocabulary to say true things about oneself. For example, in learning the vocabulary of countries, students can:

- Listen to the names of countries and repeat them
- Identify the countries they know in English, and add new ones
- Say which languages people speak in different countries
- Say which countries are near their own, or which they have personal connections with (*I'm from . . . ; My brother lives in . . . ,* etc.), or which they would like to visit

At this point, a useful step is to take time to organize the new vocabulary in some way that allows students to "notice" and bring together the target words as the basis for a communicative activity or to have a clear record for review purposes, or both. Students often write translations above new words in their textbook and these can be spread around the page; an organizing activity like the one shown in Figure 8 helps systematize their note taking and provides further personalized practice.

Complete the chart with languages and countries.
Compare your answers with a partner.

| I can speak . . . | I can't speak . . . | I want to go to . . . |
|---|---|---|
| *Portuguese a little English* | *Korean* | *Australia* |
| | | |

**Figure 8:** A vocabulary-organizing activity.
(From *Touchstone*)

### Make vocabulary learning personal

Related to the point above, materials should provide opportunities for students to use the vocabulary meaningfully, to say and write true things about themselves and their lives. Students should be encouraged to add vocabulary they want to learn, too. And if the experience of learning is also enjoyable, so much the better! One note of caution is that personalization may be more appropriate for some students than others. In a large study of vocabulary learning strategies used by students at different ages, Schmitt (1997) reports that younger (junior high school) students found that personalization was less helpful to them than the older students in university and adult classes.

### Don't overdo it!

Another important point is not to overload students – there are limits to how much vocabulary anyone can absorb for productive use in one lesson and this will be affected by how "difficult" the words are and how much students are required to know about them [on the notion of difficulty, see Laufer (1997)]. If vocabulary sets ever seem too daunting for students, allow them to choose which items they want to prioritize.

### Use strategic vocabulary in class

Since the classroom may be the main or only place that students hear or use English, it's important to include in lessons the strategic vocabulary we identified in Part 1 (see pages 8–17), as it makes up so much of spoken vocabulary. If the textbook doesn't include this as part of the syllabus or contain presentation and practice activities like the ones on pages 14–17, it will be up to the teacher as the most experienced user of English to find ways to introduce this type of vocabulary in class. It might be useful here to look at the different types of talk that happen in classrooms, which Walsh (2006) divides into four "modes": managerial, materials, skills and systems, and classroom context, each of which has different teaching aims and can include different functions.

- **Managerial mode** refers to the way teachers organize the class and move between activities. In doing this, it's possible to use a range of basic discourse markers for starting, concluding, and changing topics, such as *All right/Okay, So, Let's start, Let's move on.*

  Although Walsh sees this type of talk primarily as the teacher's, as the one who organizes and manages what happens in the classroom, there are aspects of managerial talk that students can usefully learn to help them organize pair and group work (*OK, let's change roles; That's it, we're finished*), or to interact with the teacher in order to change the way the class proceeds (*Could you explain that again, please?*).

- **Materials mode** refers to the talk that takes place when teachers and students are doing an activity in the materials. This includes eliciting answers from students, checking and explaining answers, and giving feedback on answers. In this type of talk, it would be useful for teachers to model different kinds of responses when evaluating students' answers (*That's right; Excellent*) and when seeking clarification (*You mean . . . ?; He went where?*).

- **Skills and systems mode** is the largely teacher-directed talk that goes on when the teacher is trying to get students to use a particular language item or skill and will involve the teacher in giving feedback, explaining, and correcting. In this mode teachers can model phrases for reformulation (*I mean . . .*) and for organizing and staging information (*Now, . . . First of all, . . .*).

- **Classroom context mode** refers to the type of language learners use when they are talking about their personal experience or feelings – sometimes called "freer practice activities." Here the teacher's role is to listen and support the interaction, which is the most like casual conversation that learners will engage in. Teachers can support these "conversations" by teaching the types of strategic vocabulary identified on pages 14–17 in this booklet, in order to help students manage their own talk, relate to other students, respond, and manage the conversation as a whole.

See also McCarthy and Walsh (2003) for an overview of the four modes and the ways that teachers can teach and promote natural conversational language in class.

### Helping students become independent learners in and out of class

A lot of vocabulary learning research points to the relative success of learners who are independent, devote time to self-study, use a variety of learning strategies, and keep good vocabulary notes. As Gu (2003) summarizes his own and other studies, "Good learners seem to be those who initiate their own learning, selectively attend to words of their own choice, studiously try to remember these words, and seek opportunities to use them." We can help students be better learners and acquire good learning habits by setting structured learning tasks that can be done out of class. These might include helping students construct a vocabulary notebook, using resources such as dictionaries and the Internet, and finding opportunities to use English. Let's look at these three areas.

### Vocabulary notebooks

Materials which give space to personal learning logs, like vocabulary notebooks, encourage students to continue learning outside of class. Although learning logs are often recommended to be in loose-leaf folders or on cards and separate from the textbook (Schmitt and Schmitt 1995), the course book can play a valuable role by offering guidance in the form of different types of note-taking skills and learning tips, as well as providing organizing tools such as templates, grids, and charts. Very often students' own vocabulary note-taking consists only of writing translations of single words in lists, but it can be much more varied than this, including labeling pictures and diagrams, completing charts and word webs, writing true sentences, creating short dialogues, etc. (See the *Touchstone* series Student Books for more ideas.) Good vocabulary notebook activities show students what is worth writing down and give ideas for various ways of organizing vocabulary notes, using different grouping ideas, as mentioned above.

### Research tools

Students now have access to vast resources such as the Internet and the wealth of information in learners' and online dictionaries. If students are trained how to use these resources and understand how they can provide information on formality, collocation, grammatical patterns, etc., they can exploit these resources more effectively and become more independent in their learning.

### Everyday usage

Materials can also provide students with ideas to activate and practice vocabulary in their everyday life, which is especially useful for students who live in non-English-speaking environments. Activities might include labeling items of furniture in English in a room, or trying to remember the English name for all the items they see in a clothing store. As mentioned earlier, the act of retrieving vocabulary seems to be an effective way of learning, and such activities can take place at any point in the day – not just at times designated for studying English.

# 3 | *Concluding Remarks*

The acquisition of vocabulary is arguably the most critical component of successful language learning. Until recently, however, it has been difficult to determine the most important words and phrases needed to establish a suitable vocabulary for conducting conversations most effectively. The Corpus' massive collection of texts has given us access to a wealth of information regarding spoken and written English that was previously unavailable.

The task at hand, therefore, is to take this new information and apply it in the classroom. Since there are so many things to learn about each piece of vocabulary (meaning, spoken/written forms, collocations, connotations, grammatical behavior, etc.) it is important that we as teachers only introduce a little at a time, starting with the most frequent, useful, and learnable vocabulary, and returning later to more difficult vocabulary and less frequent uses of previously learned items. We need to repeat vocabulary often, because students must work with a word or phrase many times before acquisition takes place, and we must offer variety to keep the exercises fresh and to cater to different learning styles. Finally, we need to help students understand that learning is a gradual process that takes place in small, manageable increments over time, and to encourage them to seek additional information on their own, personalizing the learning experience and tailoring it to their own specific needs.

Jeanne McCarten
January 2007

# 4 | *Appendices*

## Top 200 spoken words

For a list of the top 500 works, see any level of *Touchstone* Teacher's Edition (McCarthy, McCarten, and Sandiford; Cambridge University Press)

| | | | | |
|---|---|---|---|---|
| 1. I | 41. with | 81. they're | 121. even | 161. five |
| 2. and | 42. he | 82. kind | 122. those | 162. always |
| 3. the | 43. one | 83. here | 123. over | 163. school |
| 4. you | 44. are | 84. from | 124. probably | 164. look |
| 5. uh | 45. this | 85. did | 125. him | 165. still |
| 6. to | 46. there | 86. something | 126. who | 166. around |
| 7. a | 47. I'm | 87. too | 127. put | 167. anything |
| 8. that | 48. all | 88. more | 128. years | 168. kids |
| 9. it | 49. if | 89. very | 129. sure | 169. first |
| 10. of | 50. no | 90. want | 130. can't | 170. does |
| 11. yeah | 51. get | 91. little | 131. pretty | 171. need |
| 12. know | 52. about | 92. been | 132. gonna | 172. us |
| 13. in | 53. at | 93. things | 133. stuff | 173. should |
| 14. like | 54. out | 94. an | 134. come | 174. talking |
| 15. they | 55. had | 95. you're | 135. these | 175. last |
| 16. have | 56. then | 96. said | 136. by | 176. thought |
| 17. so | 57. because | 97. there's | 137. into | 177. doesn't |
| 18. was | 58. go | 98. I've | 138. went | 178. different |
| 19. but | 59. up | 99. much | 139. make | 179. money |
| 20. is | 60. she | 100. where | 140. than | 180. long |
| 21. it's | 61. when | 101. two | 141. year | 181. used |
| 22. we | 62. them | 102. thing | 142. three | 182. getting |
| 23. huh | 63. can | 103. her | 143. which | 183. same |
| 24. just | 64. would | 104. didn't | 144. home | 184. four |
| 25. oh | 65. as | 105. other | 145. will | 185. every |
| 26. do | 66. me | 106. say | 146. nice | 186. new |
| 27. don't | 67. mean | 107. back | 147. never | 187. everything |
| 28. that's | 68. some | 108. could | 148. only | 188. many |
| 29. well | 69. good | 109. their | 149. his | 189. before |
| 30. for | 70. got | 110. our | 150. doing | 190. though |
| 31. what | 71. OK | 111. guess | 151. cause | 191. most |
| 32. on | 72. people | 112. yes | 152. off | 192. tell |
| 33. think | 73. now | 113. way | 153. I'll | 193. being |
| 34. right | 74. going | 114. has | 154. maybe | 194. bit |
| 35. not | 75. were | 115. down | 155. real | 195. house |
| 36. um | 76. lot | 116. we're | 156. why | 196. also |
| 37. or | 77. your | 117. any | 157. big | 197. use |
| 38. my | 78. time | 118. he's | 158. actually | 198. through |
| 39. be | 79. see | 119. work | 159. she's | 199. feel |
| 40. really | 80. how | 120. take | 160. day | 200. course |

# Further reading

## On corpus issues

For an introduction to the use of a corpus in *Touchstone* and other materials, read *Touchstone: From Corpus to Course Book,* by Michael McCarthy, in this series.

See also *Explorations in Corpus Linguistics* for papers by Michael McCarthy and Ronald Carter on fluency, clusters in conversation, and spoken grammar, also in this series.

To read more about how corpus information can inform classroom materials and teaching, see *From Corpus to Classroom* by Anne O'Keeffe, Michael McCarthy, and Ronald Carter, published by Cambridge University Press.

## On vocabulary

*Vocabulary: Description, Acquisition and Pedagogy* edited by Norbert Schmitt and Michael McCarthy, *Learning Vocabulary in Another Language* by Paul Nation and *Vocabulary in Language Teaching* by Norbert Schmitt, all published by Cambridge University Press give excellent coverage of vocabulary teaching and learning issues.

For a general overview of vocabulary learning research see Peter Gu's article: Vocabulary Learning in a Second Language: Person, Task, Context and Strategies. TESL–EJ 7: 2 http://www-writing.berkeley.edu/tesl-ej/ej26/a4.html

# References

Carter, R. A., and M. J. McCarthy (1995). Grammar and the spoken language. *Applied Linguistics* 16(2):141–158.

Carter, R. A., and M. J. McCarthy (2006). *Cambridge Grammar of English.* Cambridge: Cambridge University Press.

Francis, W. N., and H. Kucera (1982). *Frequency analysis of English Usage.* Boston : Houghton Mifflin Company.

Ghadirian, S. (2002). Providing controlled exposure to target vocabulary through the screening and arranging of texts. *Language, Learning & Technology* 6 (1):147–164.

Global Language Monitor. http://www.languagemonitor.com/GlobalLanguageMonitor.html

Goulden, R., P. Nation, and J. Read (1990). How large can a receptive vocabulary be? *Applied Linguistics 11* (4):341–63

Gu, P. Y. (2003). Vocabulary Learning in a Second Language: Person, Task, Context and Strategies. *TESL–EJ 7*:2.

Laufer, B. (1997). What's in a word that makes it hard or easy: Some intralexical factors that affect the learning of words. In Schmitt, N., and M. J. McCarthy (Eds.) (1997). *Vocabulary: Description, Acquisition and Pedagogy*. Cambridge: Cambridge University Press, 140–155.

McCarthy, M. J. (2004). *Touchstone: From Corpus to Course Book* Cambridge: Cambridge University Press.

McCarthy, M. J., and R. A. Carter (2002). This, that and the other: Multiword clusters in spoken English as visible patterns of interaction. *Teanga: The Irish Yearbook of Applied Linguistics*, vol. 21. Reprinted in *Explorations in Corpus Linguistics* Cambridge University Press, in this series.

McCarthy, M., and S. Walsh (2003). Discourse In Nunan D. (Ed.) (2003). *Practical English Language Teaching*. New York: McGraw-Hill, 173–195.

McCarthy, M. J., J. McCarten, and H. Sandiford (2005, 2006). *Touchstone* Student Books and Teacher's Editions Levels 1–4. Cambridge: Cambridge University Press.

Melka, F. (1997). Receptive vs. productive aspects of vocabulary. In Schmitt, N., and M. J. McCarthy (Eds.) (1997). *Vocabulary: Description, Acquisition and Pedagogy*. Cambridge: Cambridge University Press, 84–102.

Merriem Webster Online, http://www.m-w.com/help/faq.htm

Nation, I. S. P. (1990). *Teaching and Learning Vocabulary*. New York: Newbury House.

Nation, I. S. P. (2001). *Learning Vocabulary in Another Language*. Cambridge: Cambridge University Press.

O'Dell, F. (1997). Incorporating vocabulary into the syllabus. In Schmitt, N., and M. J. McCarthy (Eds.) (1997). *Vocabulary: Description, Acquisition and Pedagogy*. Cambridge: Cambridge University Press, 258–278.

O'Keeffe, A., M. J. McCarthy, and R. A. Carter (2007). *From Corpus to Classroom*. Cambridge: Cambridge University Press.

Rott, S. (1999). The effect of exposure frequency on intermediate language learners' incidental vocabulary acquisition and retention through reading. *Studies in Second Language Acquisition* 21:589–619.

Schmitt, N. (1997). Vocabulary Learning Strategies. In Schmitt, N., and M. J. McCarthy (Eds.) (1997). *Vocabulary: Description, Acquisition and Pedagogy*. Cambridge: Cambridge University Press, 199–227.

Schmitt, N. (2000). *Vocabulary in Language Teaching*. Cambridge: Cambridge University Press.

Schmitt, N. and D. Schmitt (1995). Vocabulary notebooks: Theoretical underpinnings and practice suggestions. *ELT Journal* 49(2):133–143.

Schmitt, N., and M. J. McCarthy (Eds.) (1997). *Vocabulary: Description, Acquisition and Pedagogy.* Cambridge: Cambridge University Press.

Sökmen, A. (1997). Current trends in teaching second language vocabulary. In Schmitt, N., and M. J. McCarthy (Eds.) (1997). *Vocabulary: Description, Acquisition and Pedagogy.* Cambridge: Cambridge University Press, 237–257.

Tomlinson, B. (Ed.) (1998). *Materials Development in Language Teaching.* Cambridge: Cambridge University Press.

Walsh, S. (2006). *Investigating Classroom Discourse.* London: Routledge.

Wilkins, D. (1972). *Linguistics in Language Teaching.* London: Edward Arnold.